FROM BEGINNER TO CHEF

Simply Creative Cooking

FROM BEGINNER TO CHEF

Simply Creative Cooking

Nishat Pestonji

Popular Prakashan
www.popularprakashan.com

Published by
POPULAR PRAKASHAN PVT. LTD.
301, Mahalaxmi Chambers
22, Bhulabhai Desai Road
Mumbai – 400 026

First Published 2011

(4412)
ISBN: 978-81-7991-664-3

Design: Anjali Sawant
Layout: Satyawan Rane
Photography: Arvind Sawant
Sketches: Mulchand Panchal

Printed in India
by Saurabh Printers Pvt. Ltd.
A-16, Sector 4, Noida

Contents

Introduction

My daughters were in their early teens when I went on strike. Not a hunger strike for some moral cause but a labour strike – in our own home! Zany…? Not quite….

It happened this way. The girls were going through a difficult adolescence in a single-parent household with me struggling to establish myself as a journalist while battling on several family fronts. Living with us was not easy. Three maids quit within weeks. While the third one was packing up I overheard the girls celebrating 'Yeay! Now we'll get Mummy *ka hath ka khaana*'.

"Did I hear right?" I asked, aghast that they'd been plotting to get rid of the maid. As if I didn't have my hands full enough!

They nodded gleefully, expecting me to be flattered. "Make yummy Ham and Rice tomorrow, Mamma."

"Pl-ea-ease."

"I am not entering the kitchen," said I firmly.

"You have an assignment….? We can get food from outside."

"Make your delicious Chicken Casserole over the weekend."

They'd missed the glare in my eyes.

"Girls," I said, gritting my teeth. "I am not entering the kitchen from tomorrow onwards. Not tomorrow, not the weekend, not next week."

Something was beginning to register. "Then…then who'll cook?", stammered Nishat.

"You!"

"Me?!!!!"

"Yes, you and Naheed."

"But…but we can't…"

"We don't know how to cook, Mamma."

"You'll have to learn or we're all going to starve. From now I will not enter the kitchen till you two can serve up a decent meal."

Thus began the culinary lessons with me doing nothing more than giving verbal instructions. The first few days we survived on *puch-puch chawal* and *kali (burnt) dal.*

I remained unrelenting. No outside food.

When stocks ran out I bought vegetables, rice, *dal*, fish. No quick bites. Not even biscuits, *chivda* or cheese. By the fourth day the rice and *dal* were beginning to look like rice and *dal*, though the *dal* still had no *tadka*.

Then Naheed tentatively asked "Can I try chips? We have ketchup in the fridge."

"Okay," said I, slightly apprehensive, for lowering wet potatoes into hot oil can be tricky for a beginner.

"Will you cut potatoes for me?"

"The peeler and knife are in the drawer."

"If I cut my hand....?"

"There's a first time for everyone. Be careful."

Some potato wedges were thick, some were thin. Naheed pan-fried instead of deep-frying. But the chips tasted good after the gooey stuff we'd survived on. One week into my labour strike we had not-brilliantly-cooked-but-edible French fries. That was the beginning.

The repertoire increased. Chips were accompanied by fried fish. Eggs were boiled, fried, scrambled. *Dal* and rice combined into a *khichdi*. I had graduated from 'cook' to 'teacher'. It was time to re-enter the kitchen.

Nishat took longer than Naheed to get over her fear of getting burnt. When it was her turn to cook, she'd get Naheed to light the gas stove and stretch over the *degchi* from two feet away with a long-handled spoon! Since she wears loose kaftans there was a risk of her clothes catching fire unless she did things properly.

I decided to teach her to make White Sauce which requires constant stirring. Holding her hand, I forced her to stir, despite cries of "You're going to kill me!" When Baked Chicken was served at a party and Nishat received compliments, her tears turned into smiles.

To widen their repertoire I decided to teach each girl to master a simple basic recipe, then go into variations that could emerge from it. That way they were quickly equipped for party cooking, and compliments are the biggest incentive for further experimentation. Nishat's White Sauce had variations in a range of baked casseroles. Naheed specialised in both Tomato and Green Chutneys from which a variety of vegetarian and non-vegetarian dishes would emerge.

This was a time when our home was a buzz of activity with theatre persons, artists, poets, and political activists coming in and out. They became our guinea-pigs, a source of suggestions and encouragement, their fast-emptying plates being our greatest compliments. Then someone had an idea. Why not supply snacks for art openings and parties?

In the eighties, art openings were modest affairs compared to today. Our venture called Creative Cuisine supplied Chicken Liver Kebabs and Potato Cheese Balls for an Akbar Padamsee opening, Paneer Salad Sandwiches and Peanut Dip for crisps at a poetry evening hosted by Adil Jussawalla, Chicken in Tangy Cheese Sauce and Jardaloo Sali Boti for boat parties arranged by A.D. Singh.

This book is the culmination of those years when the three of us muddled together to come out on top – for a while. All ventures have a life-span.... Then new adventures begin....

Meher Pestonji

Measures

1 cup = 200 ml

1 tablespoon = 15 ml

1 teaspoon = 5 ml

CHEESE SAUCE CHARMERS

The universal favourite creamy cheese sauce can convert plain fish, chicken, or vegetables into delicious casseroles.

CHEESE SAUCE

2 tablespoons butter

2 tablespoons refined flour

2 cups milk

2 x 25g processed cheese cubes, grated

1 egg, beaten

Salt to taste

Melt the butter in a pan on a low heat.

Add flour and fry for a few seconds. Slowly add the milk, stirring continuously, to make sure there are no lumps.

Add the grated cheese, beaten egg and salt. Stir till the sauce is thick.

VEGETABLES AU GRATIN

1 recipe CHEESE SAUCE

2-3 medium carrots

2 large potatoes

10-15 French beans

½ cup shelled green peas

⅓ cup dried breadcrumbs

¾ tablespoon butter

Salt to taste

Preheat the oven to 180°C/350°F/Gas Mark 4.

Chop the vegetables into cubes.

Boil carrots and potatoes in plenty of salted water till half done. Add French beans and green peas and boil till all the vegetables are tender. Drain.

Add the cooked vegetables to the cheese sauce and mix well.

Pour into a 7x9-inch oval or 8-inch square ovenproof dish and sprinkle breadcrumbs. Dot with butter and bake for 15-20 minutes till the top is golden brown. Serve hot.

BAKED CAULIFLOWER

1 recipe CHEESE SAUCE

½ kg cauliflower

¼ teaspoon pepper powder

¼ teaspoon mustard powder

⅓ cup dried breadcrumbs

1 tablespoon butter

Salt to taste

Preheat the oven to 180°C/350°F/Gas Mark 4.

Separate the cauliflower into florets. Boil in salted water till half cooked. Drain.

Pour the cheese sauce into a bowl and add cauliflower, pepper powder and mustard powder. Stir well to mix.

Transfer to an 8-inch square ovenproof dish, sprinkle with breadcrumbs, dot with butter and bake for 15-20 minutes till the top is golden brown. Serve hot.

Note

You can replace half the cauliflower with cooked pasta such as macaroni.

CHICKEN IN TANGY CHEESE SAUCE

1 recipe CHEESE SAUCE
1 kg chicken, cut into 8 pieces
100 grams corn kernels
100 grams fresh button mushrooms
1 tablespoon tomato ketchup
½ teaspoon soy sauce
½ teaspoon chilli sauce
½ teaspoon Worcestershire sauce
⅓ cup dried breadcrumbs
1 tablespoon butter
Salt to taste

Boil and shred the chicken. Discard the skin and bones. Boil the corn separately. Chop the mushrooms.

Preheat the oven to 180°C/350°F/Gas Mark 4.

Pour the cheese sauce into a bowl. Add ketchup, soy sauce, chilli sauce and Worcestershire sauce and mix well. Taste and adjust the flavours.

Add shredded chicken, corn and mushrooms to the tangy cheese sauce and mix well.

Pour into an 8-inch square or 7x9-inch ovenproof dish, sprinkle breadcrumbs, dot with butter and bake for 15-20 minutes. Serve hot.

CASSEROLE ROYALE

2 recipes CHEESE SAUCE
½ kg broccoli
200 grams mushrooms
200 grams baby corn
2 yellow capsicums
2 red capsicums
50 grams butter + 2 tablespoons
1 cup penne pasta
1 teaspoon olive oil
200 grams bean sprouts
100 grams cherry tomatoes
2 eggs
⅓ cup dried breadcrumbs

Preheat the oven to 180°C/350°F/Gas Mark 4.

Chop broccoli into pieces.

Cut mushrooms, baby corn and yellow and red capsicums into thin, long strips.

Fry each of the chopped vegetables separately, in butter, in a *kadai*. Remove and set aside.

Boil penne in plenty of boiling salted water till *al dente* (cooked but still firm to the bite). Drain and mix with 1 teaspoon of olive oil to make sure it doesn't stick.

Transfer the cheese sauce to a large bowl. Add the penne, stirring gently so that the pasta does not break.

Stir in the fried vegetables, bean sprouts and cherry tomatoes gently.

Grease a large 9x13-inch ovenproof dish with 1 tablespoon of butter. Pour the vegetable and cheese mixture into the dish.

Beat eggs lightly with a fork and pour over the top. Sprinkle with breadcrumbs to make a crisp crust, dot with 1 tablespoon butter and bake for 30 minutes. Serve hot.

FISH CASSEROLE

1 recipe CHEESE SAUCE

6 slices (450 grams) fleshy white fish (pomfret, *rawas* or seer fish)

¼ teaspoon pepper powder

1 tablespoon butter

⅓ cup dried breadcrumbs

Wash the fish and cook in a little water for a few minutes till tender. Drain and shred the fish, discarding bones and skin.

Preheat the oven to 180°C/350°F/Gas Mark 4.

Mix shredded fish and pepper powder into the cheese sauce.

Grease an 8-inch square ovenproof dish with ½ tablespoon butter. Pour in the fish and cheese sauce and sprinkle breadcrumbs over the top to form a crust. Dot with remaining butter.

Bake for 15-20 minutes till the top is golden brown. Serve hot.

BACON, MUSHROOM, AND CORN CASSEROLE

1 recipe CHEESE SAUCE

250 grams bacon slices

1 packet (200 grams) button mushrooms, thinly sliced

250 grams corn kernels, boiled

¼ teaspoon pepper powder

⅓ cup dried breadcrumbs

1 tablespoon butter

Preheat the oven to 180°C/350°F/Gas Mark 4.

Cut the fat from the bacon, and then cut the lean parts into cubes.

Fry bacon fat in a *kadai,* till golden brown, then remove from the *kadai* with a slotted spoon. Add the chopped lean bacon and fry till crispy brown. Remove and drain.

Add bacon, mushrooms, corn and pepper powder to the cheese sauce and mix well.

Pour the mixture into an 8-inch square or 7x9-inch ovenproof dish. Sprinkle breadcrumbs, dot with butter and bake for 15-20 minutes. Serve hot.

CHEESE AND WALNUT SOUFFLÉ

1 recipe CHEESE SAUCE

100 grams walnut kernels

2 eggs

Preheat the oven to 200°C/400°F/Gas Mark 6.

Grind walnuts to a fine powder.

Separate egg yolks from the egg whites and mix the yolks into the cheese sauce.

Whip the egg whites in a clean, dry bowl until stiff and they stand up in peaks.

Fold the egg white gently into the cheese sauce. Gently fold in the ground walnuts.

Transfer the mixture to an 8-inch square ovenproof dish and place immediately in the oven.

Bake for 10-15 minutes till puffed up and the top is golden. Serve at once.

TOMATO CHUTNEY TEMPTERS

You can rely on the tomato to add a tang to almost anything you cook. A tomato chutney becomes the base for unlimited improvisation.

TOMATO CHUTNEY

1 kg tomatoes

1 tablespoon oil

1 teaspoon mustard seeds

6-7 cloves garlic, peeled

4-5 dried Kashmiri chillies, broken into large bits

2 teaspoons grated jaggery

Salt to taste

Wash the tomatoes and place them in hot water for 2 minutes. Cool and remove the skin.

Heat oil in a pan; add mustard seeds. When they splutter, add garlic and dried chillies and fry for 1 minute.

Add tomatoes and salt. With a wooden spoon break up the tomato pieces. Stir in the jaggery.

Bring to a boil, lower the heat and simmer till the mixture thickens. Remove from heat. Discard chillies.

Serve as a savoury topping on salt biscuits or with bread sticks, nachos, fried fish, cutlets, or kebabs.

TOMATO PULAO

1 recipe TOMATO CHUTNEY

2-3 cups rice

2 tablespoons oil

3 onions, thinly sliced

4-5 cardamoms

2-3 x 1-inch cinnamon sticks

5-6 cloves

5-6 black peppercorns

Salt to taste

Remove the dried chillies from the tomato chutney and purée the chutney in a blender.

Clean and wash the rice.

Heat oil in a pan and fry the onions until translucent. Add cardamoms, cinnamon, cloves and peppercorns and fry for a few seconds.

Add rice by the handful, stirring continuously. Add puréed tomato chutney, salt and 4 cups water.

Bring to a boil lower the heat and cook, covered till the rice is tender.

Note

To make a non-vegetarian Tomato Pulao, add half a recipe of cooked Tomato Chicken (page 26) to the rice and cook till the rice is tender.

SWEET AND SOUR TOMATO DIP

1 recipe TOMATO CHUTNEY

Cool the chutney, remove the dried chillies, and purée in a blender.

Serve as a dip with wafers or other crisps.

TOMATO-PAR-EENDU

Eggs on Tomatoes

1 recipe TOMATO CHUTNEY

¾ tablespoon oil

2 onions, chopped

6 eggs

Salt to taste

Heat the oil in a *kadai* or frying pan and fry the onions lightly till they turn translucent.

Spread the thick tomato chutney over the onions.

Make 6 hollows in the tomato chutney, and crack one egg into each hollow.

Sprinkle salt over the eggs.

Cover and cook on low heat till the eggs set. Serve hot.

BAKED CHICKEN LIVER RISOTTO

1 recipe TOMATO CHUTNEY
¼ kg chicken liver
2 tablespoons oil
3 onions, finely chopped
5 cardamoms
2-3 x 1-inch cinnamon sticks
6-7 black peppercorns
6-7 cloves
2 cups rice
3 x 25g processed cheese cubes, grated
Salt to taste

Remove the dried chillies from the tomato chutney and purée the chutney in a blender.

Wash the chicken liver and boil in water to cover with a little salt. Drain and mash the liver with a fork.

Heat the oil in a pan and fry the onions till they turn translucent. Add cardamoms, cinnamon, peppercorns and cloves and fry for two minutes.

Add rice and stir till dry.

Add tomato chutney, mashed chicken liver and 3½ cups water and stir gently. Cook, covered, till the rice is tender.

Preheat the oven to 200°C/400°F/Gas Mark 6.

Transfer the rice to an 8-inch square ovenproof dish. Smooth the top and sprinkle grated cheese over it.

Bake for 10 minutes and serve immediately.

TOMATO CHICKEN

1 recipe TOMATO CHUTNEY

1 kg chicken, cut into medium pieces

2-3 tablespoons oil

2-3 onions, finely chopped

2 teaspoons ginger-garlic paste

Salt to taste

Remove the dried chillies from the tomato chutney and purée the chutney in a blender.

Wash the chicken.

Heat oil in a pan, and fry onions till they turn translucent. Add ginger-garlic paste and fry for a few seconds.

Add the chicken, and cook, stirring continuously, till evenly brown on all sides.

Stir in the puréed tomato chutney and salt. Cover the pan and allow chicken to cook till tender.

Serve hot, with rice or bread.

Note

This dish can also be made with fish or mutton.

KHEEMA CAPERS

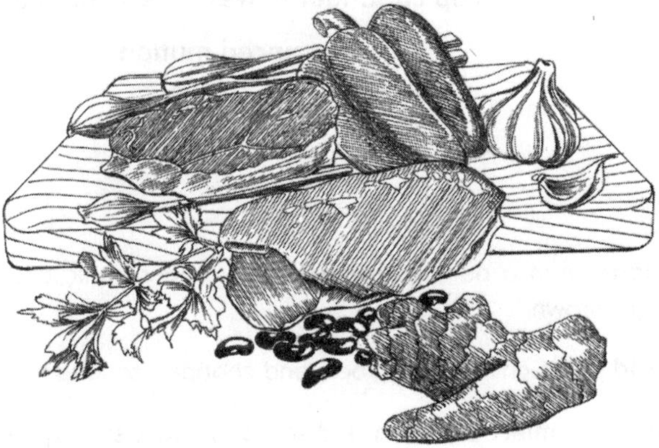

Once you have cooked the kheema there's no reason why it shouldn't take on an exotic persona. So give vent to your creative juices and unleash the gourmet in you.

SPICED MINCED MUTTON

Kheema

2 tablespoons oil

2 medium onions, finely chopped

1 teaspoon ginger-garlic paste

5-6 green chillies, finely chopped

2 tomatoes, finely chopped

½ cup coriander leaves, finely chopped

½ kg minced mutton

Salt to taste

Heat oil in a pan; add onions and ginger-garlic paste and stir till light brown.

Add green chillies, tomatoes, and chopped coriander and stir to mix.

Add the minced mutton and salt and cook, stirring continuously till it browns all over.

Add 1½ cups warm water and cook, covered, till the meat is tender and soft.

KHEEMA-PAR-EENDU

Eggs on Minced Mutton

½ recipe SPICED MINCED MUTTON

4 eggs

¼ teaspoon red chilli powder

Salt to taste

Spread the minced mutton in a large frying pan.

Make 4 hollows in the minced mutton, and crack one egg into each hollow.

Sprinkle chilli powder and salt over the eggs and cover the pan. Cook for 5 minutes on low heat till the eggs set. Serve hot.

KHEEMA CUTLETS

1 recipe SPICED MINCED MUTTON

2 slices bread

2 eggs

1 cup dried breadcrumbs

Oil for shallow-frying

Soak the bread slices in water, remove and squeeze out the water.

Add bread and 1 egg to the minced mutton.

Shape into flat oval cutlets with your hands. Beat the remaining egg.

Dip the cutlets in the beaten egg and coat with breadcrumbs.

Heat oil in a frying pan, and fry the cutlets on both sides till golden brown.

Serve with tomato ketchup.

TIRANGA PULAO

1 recipe SPICED MINCED MUTTON

1 recipe GREEN CORIANDER CHUTNEY (page 42)

3-4 cups Steamed Rice (page 78)

⅓ cup dried breadcrumbs

Preheat the oven to 200°C/400°F/Gas Mark 6.

Spread half the minced mutton in an 8-inch square transparent ovenproof dish. Press down the minced mutton with a spoon.

Spread half the rice in a layer over the mince. Press down again.

Spread a thin layer of chutney over the rice.

Spread another layer of rice over the chutney.

Spread another layer of the mince over the rice.

Sprinkle breadcrumbs and bake for 10-15 minutes. Serve hot.

MEAT LOAF

1 recipe SPICED MINCED MUTTON
2 tablespoons chilli sauce
1 tablespoon soy sauce
2 tablespoons Worcestershire sauce
2 tablespoons tomato ketchup
1 tablespoon brown vinegar
¼ kg minced bacon
3 onions, finely chopped
2 eggs, beaten
1 teaspoon pepper powder
⅓ cup dried breadcrumbs
150 grams bacon strips
Salt to taste

Preheat the oven to 200°C/400°F/Gas Mark 6.

Place the spiced minced mutton in a bowl. Add all the sauces, ketchup and vinegar, bacon mince, onions, eggs, salt and pepper powder.

Add enough breadcrumbs to bind the mixture. Taste and adjust flavour.

Grease a deep, rectangular, ovenproof loaf dish. Pack the mixture into it tightly.

Cover the top with strips of bacon and bake for 25-30 minutes. Remove from the oven and leave to cool.

Cool and turn upside down to unmould. Cut into slices and serve with a salad.

Note

This recipe also tastes good without the bacon. Meat loaf makes a tasty filling for sandwiches or a topping on toast or salt biscuits.

HAWAIIAN DELIGHT

Papaya Stuffed with Minced Mutton

1 recipe cooked SPICED MINCED MUTTON

1½-2 kg almost ripe papaya

⅓ cup dried breadcrumbs

Salt to taste

Cut the papaya in half. Remove seeds. Scoop out the flesh, leaving a ½-inch thick shell all around.

Purée the papaya in a blender, add to the minced mutton and cook on a low heat till the papaya is absorbed into the mince. Adjust the seasoning.

Preheat the oven to 200°C/400°F/Gas Mark 6.

Stuff the mince mixture into the scooped out papaya. Sprinkle breadcrumbs on top.

Grease a large ovenproof dish and place the two papaya halves in it. Bake for 10-15 minutes. Serve hot.

VEGETARIAN HAWAIIAN DELIGHT

Papaya Stuffed with Mixed Sprouts

1 tablespoon oil

1 large onion, chopped

¼ teaspoon turmeric powder

¼ teaspoon cumin powder

¼ teaspoon red chilli powder

¼ teaspoon coriander powder

2 medium tomatoes, chopped

½ kg mixed sprouted beans

1½-2 kg almost ripe papaya

½ cup dried breadcrumbs

Salt to taste

Heat oil in a pan; add chopped onion and fry till light brown. Add turmeric powder, cumin powder, chilli powder and coriander powder and fry till dry. Add tomatoes and sprouted beans and cook till the beans are tender. Season with salt.

Cut the papaya in half. Remove seeds. Scoop out the flesh, leaving a thin shell all around.

Purée papaya pulp in a blender and add to the sprouts. Cook on low heat till the papaya is absorbed.

Preheat the oven to 200°C/400°F/Gas Mark 6.

Stuff the mixture into the scooped out papaya. Sprinkle the breadcrumbs on top.

Grease a large ovenproof dish and place the papaya halves in it. Bake for 10-15 minutes. Serve hot.

MASHED POTATO MASQUERADE

The English may swear by 'Sausages and Mash', but mashed potato is far more versatile, and can be combined with almost anything you choose. Shaped and re-shaped, flavoured with condiments till it ceases to look like itself.

MASHED POTATO

4 medium potatoes

1-2 tablespoons butter

Salt to taste

Boil the potatoes, peel and mash with a fork or potato masher while hot.

Add salt and butter and mix till smooth.

CHEESY MASHED POTATO

1 recipe MASHED POTATO

2 tablespoons butter

½ cup milk

2 tablespoons grated processed cheese

Salt and pepper to taste

Add, butter, milk, grated cheese, salt and pepper to the mashed potato, and mix well. Serve hot.

NISHAT'S SHEPHERD'S PIE

1 recipe MASHED POTATO
200 grams bacon, chopped
200 grams ham, chopped
1 tablespoon oil
200 grams chicken or pork sausages
3 medium onions, cut into thin rings
3 medium tomatoes, cut into thin round slices
1-2 tablespoons butter
2 hard-boiled eggs, cut into round slices
¼ teaspoon pepper powder
1 egg, beaten
Salt to taste

Preheat the oven to 200°C/400°F/Gas Mark 6.

Heat oil in a frying pan; fry the bacon and remove from the pan with a slotted spoon. Add the sausages, fry till brown, remove and slice.

Fry ham in the same oil and remove. Fry the onion rings and tomatoes.

Grease an 8-inch square ovenproof dish, with butter. Line it with the mashed potato, reserving some mashed potato to cover the pie.

Arrange the sausage, ham, bacon, onions, tomatoes, and hard-boiled eggs in the potato shell, and sprinkle pepper powder.

Cover with the remaining mashed potato.

Brush a thin layer of beaten egg on the mashed potato, and bake for 10-15 minutes till the top is golden brown.

Note

You can also fill the pie with Spiced Minced Mutton (page 28).

CORN AND CHEESE BALLS

1 recipe MASHED POTATO

100 grams American corn kernels, boiled

4 x 25-gram processed cheese cubes, grated

2 slices bread

½ cup milk

⅓ cup dried breadcrumbs or cornflakes

Oil for deep-frying

Salt to taste

Mix together the mashed potato, corn and grated cheese in a bowl.

Soak the bread in the milk. Squeeze out the milk and mix the crumbled bread into the potato mixture. Adjust seasoning.

Shape into small balls and coat with breadcrumbs or cornflakes.

Heat oil in a *kadai*. Add the cheese balls and fry till golden brown. Drain on absorbent paper and serve hot with tomato ketchup.

ALOO TIKKI

1 recipe MASHED POTATO

2 onions, finely chopped

2 teaspoons finely chopped coriander

2- 3 green chillies, finely chopped

3 eggs, beaten

⅓ cup dried breadcrumbs

Oil for shallow-frying

Salt to taste

Mix together mashed potato, onion, coriander and green chillies in a bowl. Adjust seasoning.

Shape portions into flat rounds *(tikki)* with wet or greased hands. Dip the *tikki* into beaten eggs and coat with breadcrumbs.

Heat oil in a frying pan and fry the *tikki* on both sides till golden.

BIRD'S NEST

1 recipe MASHED POTATO

1 onion, finely chopped

2-3 green chillies, finely chopped

2 teaspoons finely chopped fresh coriander

1-2 tablespoons butter for greasing

4 eggs

Pepper powder to taste

Salt to taste

Preheat the oven to 200°C/400°F/Gas Mark 6.

Mix together mashed potato, onion, chillies and chopped coriander.

Grease 4 individual ovenproof bowls with the butter, and line them with mashed potato, leaving a hollow in the centre.

Break the eggs into the hollows making sure the yolks stay intact. Sprinkle with salt and pepper powder.

Bake in the oven for 5-7 minutes till the eggs set.

POTATO PATTIES

Minced Mutton or Egg

1 recipe MASHED POTATO

2 eggs, beaten

⅓ cup dried breadcrumbs

Oil, for shallow-frying

For the filling, use any one of the following:

½ recipe SPICED MINCED MUTTON (page 28)

3-4 eggs, boiled and mashed with salt, pepper, and 1-2 tablespoons grated cheese

Take a small amount of mashed potato in your hands, and make a hollow in the centre.

Take a small quantity of any one filling and place it in the hollow, bring the edges together to enclose the filling and shape it into a patty.

Dip each patty into beaten eggs and then coat with breadcrumbs.

Heat oil in a frying pan and fry the patties on both sides till golden brown.

Serve with tomato ketchup.

CHUTNEY CREATIONS

There are as many ways of making this coriander and coconut chutney as there are fronds in a coconut tree. This is our favourite. Experiment to come up with creations of your own.

GREEN CORIANDER CHUTNEY

1 cup grated fresh coconut

1 teaspoon cumin seeds

1 teaspoon tamarind pulp

1½ cups coriander leaves

4-5 cloves garlic, peeled

1 small piece ginger

3-5 green chillies

Salt to taste

Grind all the ingredients together to a smooth paste, using very little water.

CHICKEN GREEN CURRY

1 recipe GREEN CORIANDER CHUTNEY

1 kg chicken

2 tablespoons oil

3 medium onions, finely chopped

Salt to taste

Clean and cut the chicken into 12 pieces.

Cook the chicken in a pan in 2 cups water till half-cooked. Drain and reserve the stock.

Heat the oil in a separate pan and fry onions till golden brown.

Add the chutney and stir for 2 minutes. Add the chicken, some of the reserved chicken stock and salt.

Cook on low heat till chicken is tender and the gravy is thick.

Note

You can cook mutton in the same way.

CHUTNEY SANDWICHES

1 recipe GREEN CORIANDER CHUTNEY

1 large loaf sliced bread

100 grams butter, at room temperature

Mix the chutney and butter to make a paste.

Spread the paste over bread slices, and press two slices together to make a sandwich.

Variations

Cheese and Chutney Sandwiches: add a slice of cheese to each sandwich.

Vegetable Sandwiches: add cucumber and tomato slices to each sandwich.

STUFFED POMFRET

1 recipe GREEN CORIANDER CHUTNEY

6 small pomfrets (500 grams)

¼ teaspoon turmeric powder

¼ teaspoon red chilli powder

Oil, for shallow-frying

Salt to taste

Clean the fish, remove the heads, and make a slit on the side.

Remove gills and stomach, wash, and stuff the chutney into the cavity.

Mix together the salt, turmeric powder and chilli powder and coat the outer surface of each pomfret with the mixture.

Heat the oil in a frying pan. Shallow-fry the fish on both sides till golden brown and crisp.

Serve hot, with slices of lemon.

CHUTNEY POTATO PATTIES

1 recipe GREEN CORIANDER CHUTNEY

1 recipe MASHED POTATO (page 36)

A few raisins

A few cashew nuts

2 eggs, beaten

⅓ cup dried breadcrumbs

Oil, for shallow-frying

Make small portions of the mashed potato, and flatten on your palm. Place a little chutney in the centre; add a raisin and cashew nut. Bring the edges together to enclose the stuffing. Shape into flattish round patties.

Dip the patties into the beaten eggs, then into the breadcrumbs to coat evenly on all sides.

Heat oil in a frying pan and fry the patties on both sides till golden. Serve hot.

PATRA-NI-MACHI

Fish Steamed in Banana Leaves

1 recipe GREEN CORIANDER CHUTNEY

2 medium pomfrets (500 grams)

4 banana leaves

Butter, for greasing the leaves

Salt to taste

Clean the fish, cut into slices and apply salt. Apply chutney over each piece.

Cut the banana leaves according to the size of the fish, grease one side with butter and wrap individual pieces of the fish in it.

Place in a double boiler, or in a covered perforated container over a pan of boiling water, and steam for 7 to10 minutes.

Serve immediately with lemon wedges.

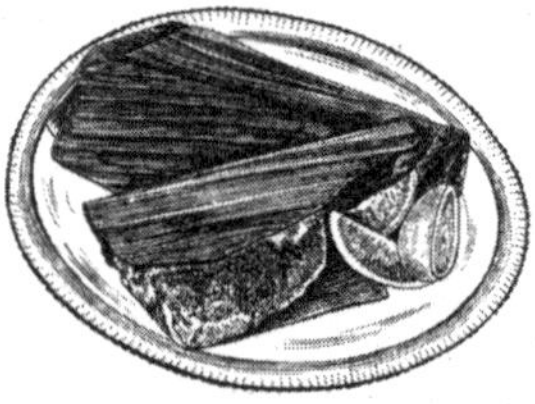

MAYONNAISE MARVELS

Mayonnaise adds personality and pizazz to a dish.

MAYONNAISE

½ teaspoon pepper powder

½ teaspoon sugar

½ teaspoon mustard powder

2 eggs

½ small potato, boiled and chopped

¾ cup olive oil

½ teaspoon salt

Place pepper powder, salt, sugar, mustard powder, and eggs in a blender with the potato and blend at a low speed.

Add olive oil drop by drop, blending continuously, till it reaches the consistency of a thick sauce.

Transfer to a bottle and store in a refrigerator.

Makes 1 cup

Note

Potato is used in this version of mayonnaise to cut down on the amount of oil.

RUSSIAN SALAD

1 recipe MAYONNAISE

2 medium carrots

2 medium potatoes

A few French beans

½ cup shelled green peas

A few lettuce leaves

Salt to taste

Cut the carrots and potatoes into small cubes.

String the French beans and cut into small pieces.

Boil carrots and potatoes, in plenty of water, in a pan. When half done, add French beans and green peas and cook till tender. Drain and cool.

Mix the cooled vegetables well with mayonnaise, taste for salt and refrigerate.

Transfer to a salad bowl lined with lettuce leaves and serve cold.

STUFFED EGGS

3-4 tablespoons MAYONNAISE

6 hard-boiled eggs

½ teaspoon mustard powder

½ teaspoon pepper powder

6 olives, halved, for garnishing

Salt to taste

Peel the eggs and halve them lengthways. Remove the yolks, leaving the whites intact.

Mash the egg yolks in a small bowl. Add the mustard powder, pepper powder, salt and mix.

Add enough mayonnaise to make a thick paste.

Fill the paste into the egg whites. You can also pipe the stuffing into the egg whites with an icing bag and a star nozzle. Garnish with olives and serve.

Note

Stuffed eggs can be used to decorate a variety of salads.

PRAWN COCKTAIL

¾ cup MAYONNAISE

250 grams small prawns, peeled and deveined

½ cup spring onions, chopped

1 teaspoon Worcestershire sauce

½ teaspoon red chilli sauce

¼ teaspoon Tabasco sauce, or to taste

Salt to taste

Place the prawns with salt in a pan; add water to cover. Cook till pink. Drain.

Cool the prawns and mix together with chopped spring onions.

Mix together the mayonnaise, Worcestershire sauce, chilli sauce and Tabasco sauce. Taste and adjust seasoning.

Mix in the prawns and spoon into cocktail glasses and refrigerate.

Serve cold.

TARTARE SAUCE

1 recipe MAYONNAISE

2-3 celery stalks, finely chopped

2 spring onion green stalks, finely chopped

½ medium tomato, finely chopped

Place mayonnaise in a bowl. Add the chopped celery, spring onion greens, tomato and mix well. Serve cold.

Note

Tartare sauce is traditionally served with Crumb-Fried Fish (page 94).

FISH MAYONNAISE

1½ recipes MAYONNAISE

6 pomfret fillets (500 grams)

A bunch of lettuce leaves, thinly sliced

2 tomatoes, sliced

1 cucumber, sliced

1 recipe Stuffed Eggs (page 50), optional

Salt and pepper, to taste

Steam the fish fillets with salt and pepper till tender. Drain and cool.

Spread the sliced lettuce on an attractive flat dish.

Arrange the fish fillets on the lettuce.

Pour the mayonnaise over the fillets.

Garnish with tomato slices, cucumber slices and stuffed eggs.

CHICKEN MAYONNAISE

1 recipe MAYONNAISE

1 kg chicken, cut into 8-10 pieces

2 teaspoons ginger-garlic paste

¾ cup finely chopped spring onions

¼ cup finely chopped celery

A few lettuce leaves

1 pomegranate, separated into kernels

Salt to taste

Rub the chicken with ginger-garlic paste. Place in a deep pan with water to cover, add salt, and boil till tender. Cool and shred the chicken. Discard the skin and bones.

Mix together the shredded chicken, spring onions, and celery, in a bowl. Add the mayonnaise and mix well.

Spread the mixture over the lettuce leaves.

Sprinkle with pomegranate kernels on top and refrigerate.

Serve cold.

Variations

Chicken Pineapple Mayonnaise: Add finely chopped pineapple to the chicken mayonnaise. Decorate with pineapple slices.

Chicken Roll and Sandwiches: Line bread rolls with lettuce leaves and fill with chicken mayonnaise. Sandwich between slices of brown or white bread. Cut in triangles.

Chicken Canapés: Serve on toast or in canapé cases.

POTATO AND DILL SALAD

1 recipe MAYONNAISE

5 large potatoes

½ cup fresh dill, finely chopped

½ cup coriander leaves, finely chopped

1 cup spring onions, chopped into thin round slices

Salt to taste

Boil potatoes in plenty of salted water. Cool, peel, and cut into medium cubes.

Reserve a little chopped dill and coriander for garnishing.

Add a handful of potatoes, then a little spring onion, a little dill and coriander, one ingredient at a time, to a large bowl, and stir in the mayonnaise with a wooden spoon. Continue in the same way till all the ingredients are used up. Adjust the seasoning.

Spoon into a salad bowl and sprinkle the reserved dill and coriander on top.

Refrigerate and serve cold.

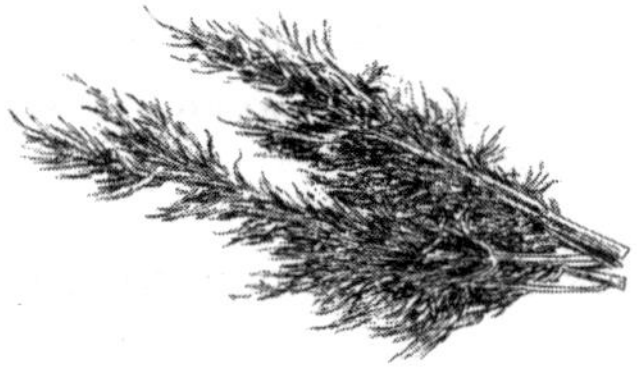

FRENCH DRESSING FLAIR

A dash of this dressing will turn any salad into a flavourful feast.

FRENCH DRESSING

½ teaspoon sugar
½ teaspoon pepper powder
½ teaspoon salt
½ teaspoon mustard powder
1 tablespoon white vinegar
2 tablespoons olive oil

Mix all the ingredients in a bowl, and stir well. Or put all the ingredients into a jar with a tight-fitting lid and shake well to mix.

Pour over salads just before serving.

Makes 4 tablespoons

GRAPE FRUIT, APPLE AND POTATO SALAD

1½ recipes FRENCH DRESSING
2 medium potatoes
100 grams corn kernels
2 medium apples
Lemon juice, as required
1 grape fruit
2 medium cucumbers
¾ cup chopped spring onions
Salt to taste

Boil the potatoes in plenty of salted water. Cool, peel and cut into cubes.

Boil the corn.

Cut apples the same size as potatoes. Sprinkle lemon juice over the apples to prevent discolouration.

Peel the grape fruit, remove membrane and seeds and cut segments into cubes.

Cut cucumbers and spring onions into round slices.

Combine all ingredients in a bowl.

Pour French dressing over the salad just before serving. Toss to mix.

BEETROOT SALAD

1 recipe FRENCH DRESSING

½ kg beetroot

1 cup sliced spring onions

5-7 celery stalks, finely chopped

Salt to taste

Boil the beetroot in plenty of salted water. Cool, peel and cut into cubes and refrigerate. Refrigerate spring onions with chopped celery.

Mix the beetroot, spring onions, and celery, just before serving.

Add French dressing, toss to mix, and serve at once.

CUCUMBER AND DILL SALAD

1 recipe FRENCH DRESSING

½ kg cucumber, cut into thin round slices

½ cup fresh dill, finely chopped

Mix the cucumber slices and dill together. Just before serving add French dressing. Toss to mix.

PASTA SALAD

2 recipes FRENCH DRESSING

¾ cup fusilli

¾ cup penne

1 tablespoon olive oil

2 red capsicums, finely chopped

2 yellow capsicums, finely chopped

1½ cups chopped spring onions

2 tomatoes, finely chopped

½ cup pomegranate kernels

Salt to taste

Boil the penne and fusilli as instructed on the packet. Drain. Add 1 tablespoon olive oil to keep them from sticking.

Mix all ingredients together, reserving half the pomegranate kernels, tossing, rather than stirring to avoid breaking the pasta. Place in a refrigerator to chill.

Pour the French dressing over the salad just before serving, and mix well with a wooden spoon. Adjust the seasoning.

Sprinkle reserved pomegranate kernels over the top. Serve at once.

DAHI DELIGHTS

Cool and nutritious as plain dahi, yoghurt brings its subtle flavour to a variety of ingredients - from the humdrum brinjal and potatoes to chicken and the most delicious sweets.

YOGHURT

½ litre milk

½ teaspoon yoghurt

Boil the milk and cool till it is lukewarm.

Rub the insides of a bowl with a little of the yoghurt. Pour in the lukewarm milk and mix the remaining yoghurt into the milk.

Leave to set in a warm dry place for 5-6 hours.

Makes 2 cups

Variations

Fruity Yoghurt: Stir chopped fresh fruit or mixed dried fruit into the yoghurt for a healthy snack.

Breakfast Booster: Serve on top of cornflakes or your favourite cereal.

MISHTI DOI

Bengali Sweet Yoghurt

1 litre milk

1½ tablespoons jaggery

1 teaspoon yoghurt

Bring the milk to a boil. Add jaggery and cook on low heat till the milk is reduced to half its original quantity.

Rub the insides of an earthenware bowl (*mitti ki handi*) with the yoghurt. Pour in the milk, and mix well.

Leave to set in a warm dry place for 5-6 hours. Serve cold.

BOONDI RAITA

1 cup chilled YOGHURT

50 grams *boondi*

¼ teaspoon red chilli powder

¼ teaspoon cumin powder

1 tablespoon chopped fresh coriander

Salt to taste

Soak the *boondi* in ½ cup warm water for 5 minutes.

Squeeze the water out of the *boondi*. Beat the yoghurt with a spoon till smooth.

Add chilli powder, cumin powder and salt to taste. Add *boondi* and mix well.

Sprinkle chopped coriander and refrigerate till ready to serve.

CUCUMBER-TOMATO RAITA

1 cup chilled YOGHURT

¼ teaspoon red chilli powder

¼ teaspoon cumin powder

1 grated cucumber or 1 finely chopped tomato, or both

Salt to taste

Beat the yoghurt lightly with a spoon till smooth. Add chilli powder, cumin powder and salt and beat again. Add cucumber and/or tomato and serve chilled.

DUM ALOO

1 cup YOGHURT

¼ kg baby potatoes

Oil for deep-frying

1 teaspoon mustard seeds

4-5 cloves garlic, finely chopped

4-5 dried Kashmiri chillies

Salt to taste

Boil the potatoes. Cool and then peel them.

Beat the yoghurt with a spoon till smooth.

Heat oil in a *kadai* and deep-fry the potatoes in small batches till golden brown. Remove potatoes with a slotted spoon and drain on absorbent paper.

Heat 1 tablespoon oil in a pan and add mustard seeds, finely chopped garlic and dried chillies. Fry till the mustard seeds start to splutter.

Add the beaten yoghurt, stirring continuously.

Add the fried potatoes and cook on a low heat till the potatoes absorb the yoghurt.

Serve hot with *chapati*.

SHAHI MURGH DAHIWALA

1½ cups YOGHURT

1 kg chicken

20 grams almonds

2 tablespoons oil

20 grams raisins

2-3 onions, finely chopped

1 teaspoon red chilli powder

1 teaspoon coriander powder

1 teaspoon cumin powder

Salt to taste

Cut the chicken into 8-10 pieces. Boil in water to cover. Drain and shred the chicken.

Soak almonds in hot water, peel and cut into strips.

Heat the oil in a pan and fry the almonds and remove. Fry the raisins and remove.

Fry the onions in the same oil, till golden brown. Add chilli powder, coriander powder, cumin powder and salt.

Mix in the yoghurt, then add the chicken. Cook on low heat for a few minutes.

Add the fried raisins and almonds.

Serve hot with rice.

KADHI

1 cup YOGHURT

1 tablespoon gram flour

1 tablespoon oil

1 teaspoon mustard seeds

2-4 cloves garlic, peeled and coarsely chopped

2-3 sprigs curry leaves

Salt to taste

Beat the yoghurt lightly with a spoon. Add gram flour and salt and mix well.

Heat oil in a *kadai*. Add mustard seeds and garlic and fry till the mustard seeds begin to splutter.

Remove curry leaves from the sprigs, and add to the oil. Fry lightly.

Add yoghurt mixture and stir well, making sure there are no lumps.

Cook on a low heat till thick, stirring occasionally. Serve hot.

PASTA PARADE

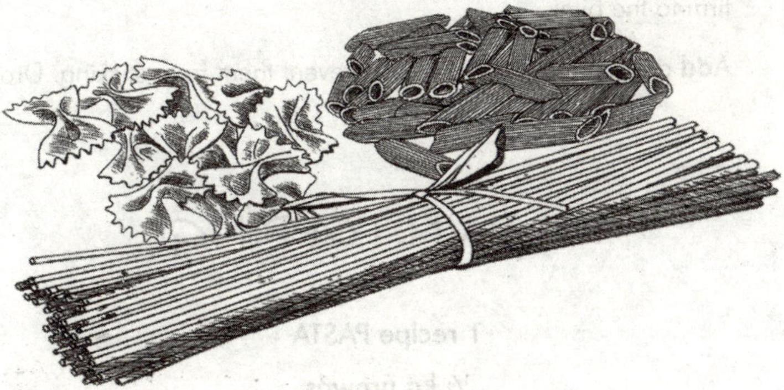

Kids love slurping snaky spaghetti and guzzling on pasta. Add toppings for flavour and fun.

PASTA

250 grams spaghetti or any other pasta

1 teaspoon olive oil

Boil plenty of water in a pan.

Add the spaghetti or pasta and cook till *al dente* (cooked but still firm to the bite).

Add a teaspoon of olive oil to prevent them from sticking. Drain.

PRAWN TOPPING

1 recipe PASTA

½ kg prawns

1½ cups spring onions

3-4 green chillies

1 tablespoon oil

1 teaspoon ginger-garlic paste

Salt to taste

Shell and devein the prawns.

Cut spring onions and green chillies into round slices.

Heat the oil in a pan and fry the spring onions, green chillies and ginger-garlic paste for 1 minute. Add prawns, and cook on low heat till done. Season with salt to taste.

Spread the pasta on a flat serving dish and spoon the prawns on top. Serve at once.

KING'S TOPPING

1 recipe PASTA

2 carrots

2 potatoes

2 capsicums

2 tomatoes

2 large onions

2 tablespoons oil

250 grams cocktail sausages

Salt to taste

Chop carrots, potatoes, capsicums, tomatoes and onions into long strips.

Heat the oil in a *kadai* and fry the sausages. Remove them from the oil and slit them lengthways.

Stir-fry all the chopped ingredients in the same oil, separately.

Mix the fried ingredients together. Season with salt to taste.

Spread the pasta on a flat serving dish and spoon the fried ingredients on top.

Serve at once.

QUEEN'S TOPPING

1 recipe PASTA

¼ kg broccoli

200 grams fresh mushrooms

2 yellow capsicums

1 red capsicum

2 green capsicums

1½ cups spring onions, cut into round slices

150 grams baby corn, slit lengthways

4 tablespoons butter

5-7 cloves garlic, peeled

Salt to taste

Chop broccoli and mushrooms. Cut all the capsicums into long thin strips.

Heat the butter in a pan, and lightly fry each of the chopped vegetables and garlic, separately. Remove, drain and mix the fried vegetables together. Season with salt to taste.

Spread the cooked pasta on a flat serving dish and spoon the vegetable mixture on top. Serve at once.

SPAGHETTI MINCE PIE

1 recipe SPAGHETTI

1 recipe SPICED MINCED MUTTON (page 28)

Line an oval 7x9-inch heatproof pie dish with the cooked spaghetti leaving the centre hollow.

Fill the centre with mince.

Seal the top with aluminium foil.

Place the dish in a larger metal pan and pour water to come up half way up the dish.

Cover the pan and steam the pie for 20 minutes. Remove the dish from the pan.

Turn the dish upside down onto a serving plate to unmould the pie. Serve hot.

SPAGHETTI BOLOGNESE

1 recipe SPAGHETTI

½ recipe SPICED MINCED MUTTON (page 28)

½ kg tomatoes

1 tablespoon oil

2 onions, finely chopped

5-6 cloves garlic, finely chopped

Grated Parmesan or processed cheese, as required

Wash the tomatoes. Boil 5-6 cups water, pour it over the tomatoes and cover with a lid.

Leave to stand for 2-3 minutes.

Drain and peel the tomatoes.

Blend the tomatoes into a thick purée.

Heat the oil in a pan; add the onions and garlic and fry till the onions turn soft and translucent.

Pour in the tomato purée and stir well to mix. Cook for 2 minutes.

Add the minced mutton and cook for a few minutes.

Transfer the spaghetti to a bowl or platter and pour the meat sauce over.

Sprinkle grated cheese and serve hot.

Note

You can also mix the meat sauce carefully into the spaghetti and serve, sprinkled with cheese.

BLENDER BOUNTY

The blender is the chef's best friend as it turns out quick, easy and delicious fare, leaving you time to enjoy with family and friends.

FRUIT MILK SHAKE

Fruit

(7-8 strawberries, 1 banana, or 1 *chickoo*)

1 cup milk

2 tablespoons sugar

A few ice cubes

Peel, and remove the seeds of the fruit. Chop.

Put all the ingredients into a blender; adjust sugar and blend until smooth.

LASSI

½ cup YOGHURT (page 60)

¼ cup water

Salt or sugar to taste

Blend all the ingredients together.

Pour into tall glasses and place in the refrigerator. Serve cold.

Variation

Fruit Lassi - add a chopped banana, mango, *chickoo*, or a few strawberries and blend.

PEANUT AND CHEESE DIP

200 grams salted peanuts, without the skin

½ teaspoon red chilli powder

2-3 x 25g processed cheese cubes, grated

1 cup milk

Crush the peanuts coarsely. Transfer into a blender with the rest of the ingredients.

Blend to a smooth paste.

Serve, as a dip with wafers or assorted crisps or raw vegetable fingers (carrots, cucumber and capsicum).

PICK-ME-UP SOUP

2-3 carrots

10-15 French beans

1 large potato

1 large onion

½ cup shelled green peas

¼ cup coriander leaves or mint leaves

Pepper powder to taste

Chicken wings or mutton bones (optional)

Salt to taste

Cut the carrots, French beans, and potato into cubes. Quarter the onions.

Boil 7-8 cups water in a pan, along with carrots, potato, French beans, onion, peas, salt and chicken wings or bones. Lower the heat, cover with a tight fitting lid and cook till the vegetables are half done.

Add coriander or mint and simmer for 20-30 minutes.

Remove the chicken wings or mutton bones and discard.

Cool and purée the mixture in a blender. It should be fairly thick. Pour back into the pan, adjust seasoning, heat and serve.

Note

Add 1-2 chicken stock cubes instead of the chicken or mutton bones.

CHICKEN LIVER PÂTÉ

2 tablespoons butter

½ kg chicken liver

3 x 25g processed cheese cubes, grated

2 tablespoons Worcestershire sauce

¾ cup milk

2 tablespoons red wine (optional)

Salt to taste

Heat butter in a pan, and fry the liver for a few minutes.

Blend together the liver, cheese, Worcestershire sauce, milk, and salt, to make a smooth paste.

Transfer to a bowl, add red wine and mix.

Serve with crisp bread such as lavash, or as a topping on garlic toast or salt biscuits.

PALAK METHI PANEER

Spinach and Fenugreek with Cottage Cheese

4 cups chopped spinach leaves *(palak)*

2 cups chopped fenugreek leaves *(methi)*

200 grams cottage cheese *(paneer)*

1 tablespoon oil

½ teaspoon mustard seeds

4-5 cloves garlic, chopped

2 large onions, chopped

1 large tomato, chopped

¼ teaspoon cumin powder

¼ teaspoon red chilli powder

Salt to taste

Wash the spinach and fenugreek leaves. Drain. Cut the cottage cheese into cubes.

Heat oil in a pan and add mustard seeds and garlic. When the seeds start to splutter, add onions and tomato, and fry for a few minutes. Add cumin powder and chilli powder and stir.

Add spinach and fenugreek, stirring continuously. Sprinkle 1 tablespoon water and cook, covered, on low heat till soft.

Cool and purée the mixture in a blender, with very little water.

Return to the pan, add cottage cheese and salt, and simmer for 2-3 minutes.

Serve hot with *chapati.*

RICE REVUE

Make everyday rice exciting with a few add-ins and dashes of imagination. Perfect for parties and holiday lunches.

STEAMED RICE

1 cup rice

½ teaspoon salt

Soak rice in 1 cup water for 20 minutes. Drain.

Place 2 cups water, rice and salt in a pan and bring to a boil.

Lower the heat, cover the pan and simmer till the water dries up. Serve hot.

COCONUT RICE

1 tablespoon oil

1 teaspoon mustard seeds

4-6 cloves garlic, peeled

3-4 dried Kashmiri chillies, broken into large bits

¼ teaspoon turmeric powder

½ coconut, grated

2 cups rice

Salt to taste

Heat the oil in a pan; add mustard seeds and garlic. When mustard seeds splutter, add the dried chillies and turmeric powder.

Stir in grated coconut and rice gradually. Add salt and 4 cups water and cook till rice is tender. Serve hot.

PEA PULAO

200 grams green peas, shelled

1 tablespoons oil

1 teaspoon cumin seeds

2-3 cardamoms

2-3 x 1-inch cinnamon sticks

3-4 cloves

4-5 black peppercorns

2-3 bay leaves

2 cups rice, washed

Salt to taste

Boil the peas with a little salt.

Heat oil and fry cumin seeds; add cardamom, cinnamon, cloves, peppercorns and bay leaves. Fry for 1 minute.

Add the rice, salt and 4 cups water and cook the rice till nearly done.

Add the green peas and cook on low heat till peas and rice are cooked. Serve hot.

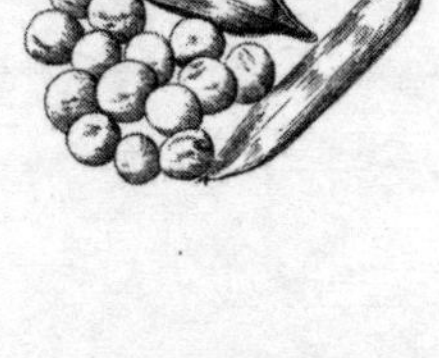

CHICKEN CAPSICUM PULAO

1 kg chicken, cut into pieces

1 cup coriander leaves, chopped

1 cup mint leaves, chopped

3- 4 capsicums

2 tablespoons oil

½ teaspoon mustard seeds

5-6 cloves garlic, peeled

2-3 green chillies

1 cup spring onions, finely chopped

2 cups rice

Salt to taste

Parboil the chicken in 4 cups of water. Drain and reserve the stock.

Purée the coriander, mint leaves, and capsicums in a blender with 1 cup reserved chicken stock.

Heat oil and fry mustard seeds till they begin to splutter. Add garlic and green chillies.

Add spring onions and fry till light brown in colour.

Add 4 cups of the coriander and mint-flavoured stock, rice and chicken and cook till the rice and chicken are tender.

Serve hot.

CELERY, HAM AND BACON PILAF

1 tablespoon oil

250 grams lean bacon, chopped

250 grams ham, chopped

2 cups spring onions, finely chopped

½ cup parsley, finely chopped

½ cup celery, finely chopped

1 cup coriander leaves, finely chopped

3 cups rice

Salt to taste

Heat oil in a pan and fry the bacon till crisp. Remove.

Fry the ham in the same oil, and remove.

Fry spring onions in the same oil, till they turn light in colour.

Add the parsley, celery, chopped coriander, and then the rice, stirring constantly.

Add the fried bacon and ham, salt to taste and 6 cups water. Cook on low heat till the rice is tender.

Serve at once.

DILL AND CORIANDER PULAO

1 cup fresh dill

1 cup coriander leaves

1 tablespoon oil

1 teaspoon mustard seeds

1-2 onions, finely chopped

3-4 green chillies, finely chopped

5-6 curry leaves

2-3 cloves garlic,

peeled and finely chopped

2 cups rice

Salt to taste

Purée the dill and coriander in a blender.

Heat oil in a pan; add the mustard seeds. When the seeds sputter, add the onions, green chillies, curry leaves and garlic, and fry for a minute.

Add rice, stirring continuously. When rice is thoroughly coated with the oil, pour in the puréed greens, salt and 4 cups water.

Cover the pan and cook till the rice is tender. Serve hot.

EGG EXTRAVAGANZA

Trust cuisine-connoisseur Parsis, to top every vegetable with eggs, sunny-side-up or whipped, and make a meal of it.

BHAAJI-PAR-EENDU

Eggs on Spinach and Fenugreek

1 tablespoons oil

1 large onion, finely chopped

1 large tomato, finely chopped

½ teaspoon red chilli powder

¼ teaspoon coriander powder

¼ teaspoon cumin powder

1 cup chopped spinach leaves

½ cup chopped fenugreek leaves

4 eggs

Salt to taste

Heat oil in a large frying pan, and fry onion and tomatoes.

Add a quarter teaspoon chilli powder, coriander powder, cumin powder and salt.

Cook till the oil separates from the *masala;* stir in the spinach and fenugreek leaves.

Beat eggs lightly and spread them over the greens covering them completely.

Sprinkle the rest of the chilli powder and a little salt and cover the frying pan.

Cook for five minutes on low heat till the eggs set. Serve hot.

BHEEDA-PAR-EENDU

Eggs on Ladies' Fingers

1 tablespoon oil

1 teaspoon mustard seeds

5-7 cloves garlic, peeled

1 large onion, finely chopped

2 medium tomatoes, finely chopped

½ kg ladies' fingers, cut into thin rounds

4 eggs

¼ teaspoon red chilli powder

Salt to taste

Heat oil in a large frying pan, and fry mustard seeds with garlic. When the mustard seeds begin to splutter, add onion and tomato.

Fry for 1 minute and add ladies' fingers and stir well. Cook till the ladies' fingers are tender.

Beat eggs lightly and spread them over the ladies' fingers, covering them completely.

Sprinkle chilli powder and salt, cover the pan and cook on low heat till the eggs set. Serve hot.

CAPSICUM-PAR-EENDU

Eggs on Capsicum

1 tablespoons oil

2-3 medium onions, finely chopped

4-5 green chillies, finely chopped

3-4 medium tomatoes, cut in round slices

4-5 medium capsicums, cut in rings

4 eggs

¼ teaspoon red chilli powder

Salt to taste

Heat oil in a large frying pan, and fry onions with green chillies.

Add tomatoes and cook, stirring, till the excess moisture dries up.

Add capsicums and salt and cook, covered, till tender.

Beat the eggs lightly and spread over the vegetables covering them completely.

Sprinkle chilli powder, salt, cover the pan and cook for five minutes on low heat till the eggs set. Serve hot.

SALI-PAR-EENDU

Eggs on Potato Straws

2 tablespoons oil

2-3 medium onions, finely chopped

4-5 green chillies, finely chopped

½ cup coriander leaves, finely chopped

250 grams thin fried potato straws

4-5 eggs

¼ teaspoon red chilli powder

Salt to taste

Heat oil in a large frying pan, and fry onions with green chillies and chopped coriander leaves.

Add potato straws and stir well.

Beat eggs lightly and spread them over the straws covering them completely, or make 6 hollows in the straws, and crack one egg into each hollow.

Sprinkle chilli powder and salt. Cover the pan and cook for 5 minutes on low heat till the eggs set. Serve hot.

PAPETA-PAR-EENDU

Eggs on Potatoes

4-5 medium potatoes

2 tablespoons oil

1 teaspoon mustard seeds

3-5 green chillies, finely chopped

4-5 cloves garlic, peeled and finely chopped

2 medium onions, sliced

¼ cup coriander leaves

¼ teaspoon turmeric powder

4-5 eggs

¼ teaspoon red chilli powder

Salt to taste

Peel potatoes and cut into thin round slices.

Heat oil in a large frying pan, and fry mustard seeds, green chillies, and garlic. Add onions and coriander leaves and fry for a few minutes.

Add potatoes, turmeric powder and salt. Cover the pan and cook till the potatoes are tender.

Beat eggs lightly, and spread them over the potatoes covering them completely.

Sprinkle chilli powder and salt, cover the pan and cook on low heat for 5 minutes till the eggs set. Serve hot.

FABULOUS FRIES

Crispy fries, the perfect light meal for a lazy afternoon. Add a salad to ease the guilt of the health-conscious.

PANEER-JEERA BALLS

4 day-old bread slices

½ cup milk

100 grams cottage cheese (*paneer*), crumbled

1 teaspoon cumin seeds

½ cup dried breadcrumbs

Oil for deep-frying

Salt to taste

Soak the bread slices in milk for a few minutes. Squeeze the milk out of the slices.

Mix together in a bowl, the cottage cheese, bread, cumin seeds and salt to taste.

Add enough breadcrumbs to form a firm mixture.

Divide the mixture into lime-sized balls.

Spread the remaining breadcrumbs on a plate, and roll the balls in the breadcrumbs.

Heat the oil in a *kadai* and deep-fry the balls till golden brown. Drain on absorbent paper.

Serve hot with tomato ketchup or Tomato Chutney (page 22).

KANDA BHAJIA

¼ kg gram flour

1 teaspoon red chilli powder

½ teaspoon turmeric powder

2 teaspoons finely chopped coriander

¼ kg onions, thinly sliced

Oil for deep-frying

½ teaspoon salt

Mix together in a bowl, the gram flour, chilli powder, turmeric powder, salt and chopped coriander with ½ cup water, to make a smooth batter.

Add onions to the batter and mix well.

Heat the oil in a *kadai*. Drop 5 or 6 teaspoonfuls of the batter at a time into the oil keeping a short distance between them to ensure they don't stick together.

Turn the *bhajia* gently while frying. Remove when golden brown and drain on absorbent paper.

Serve hot with tomato ketchup or Tomato Chutney (page 22).

Note

Instead of onions, one can also use whole large Bhavnagri green chillies, sliced potatoes, brinjals, capsicums, or cottage cheese.

CHICKEN LIVER CUTLETS

200 grams chicken liver

1 tablespoon Worcestershire sauce

1 teaspoon chilli sauce

1 teaspoon tomato ketchup

2 onions, finely chopped

2 tablespoons finely chopped coriander

1 egg, beaten

1 cup breadcrumbs

Oil for shallow-frying

Salt to taste

Place the liver in a pan; add salt and enough water to cover and cook for a few minutes till tender. Drain.

Mash the boiled liver in a bowl, with your fingers.

Add Worcestershire sauce, chilli sauce, tomato ketchup, onions, chopped coriander and egg to the mashed liver, and mix well.

Add half the breadcrumbs to the mixture, to soak up the moisture.

Shape the mixture into flat round cutlets and coat them in the remaining breadcrumbs.

Heat oil in a frying pan, and shallow-fry the cutlets till brown. Drain on absorbent paper.

Serve hot with Potato Chips (page 95) and ketchup.

CRISPY CRUMB CHOPS

6-7 mutton chops on the bone, (¼ kg) flattened

1 teaspoon ginger-garlic paste

2 tablespoons refined flour

2 eggs

2 tablespoons breadcrumbs

1 tablespoon oil

1tablespoon butter

1 teaspoon salt

Wash and pat the chops dry. Rub the ginger-garlic paste and salt into the chops and set aside to marinate for 1 hour.

Spread the refined flour on a plate. Whisk the eggs in a shallow bowl. Spread the breadcrumbs on a separate plate.

Roll each chop in the refined flour, and then dip both sides in egg.

Roll the chops in the breadcrumbs, and set aside.

Heat the oil and butter together in a frying pan. Place the chops in the pan and fry, covered, on low heat, for 10-15 minutes or until the undersides are golden brown.

Turn over the chops and fry the same way.

Insert the point of a thin knife through the chop to check if tender. Drain on absorbent paper.

Serve hot with Potato Chips (page 95).

Variation

Veal Escalopes – replace mutton chops with ¼ kg veal, cut into thin slices.

FISH AND CHIPS

Crumb-Fried Fish

6 pomfret fillets (500 grams)

2 tablespoons refined flour

2 eggs

2 tablespoons breadcrumbs

Oil for shallow-frying

1 teaspoon salt

Wash the fish fillets, rub them with 1 teaspoon salt, and set aside for 30 minutes.

Spread the flour on a plate. Whisk the eggs in a shallow bowl.

Spread the breadcrumbs on a separate plate.

Roll each fillet in flour, then dip in the egg, on both sides and roll in the breadcrumbs.

Heat the oil in a pan and fry the fillets until golden brown on both sides. Remove and drain on absorbent paper.

Serve with Potato Chips (page 95) and Tartare Sauce (page 51).

Potato Chips

3 medium potatoes, peeled and cut into thin long fingers

Oil for deep-frying

1 teaspoon salt

Soak the potato fingers in salted water for 30 minutes. Drain.

Heat the oil in a *kadai* and add the potatoes. Stir gently to ensure they do not stick to the bottom of the pan or to each other. Fry till pale gold and crisp on the outside.

Drain on absorbent paper.

Serve hot with tomato ketchup.

MUTTON KEBABS

¼ kg minced mutton

2 onions, finely chopped

1 small tomato, finely chopped

¼ cup coriander, finely chopped

2 green chillies, finely chopped

1 teaspoon ginger-garlic paste

1 egg

½ cup breadcrumbs

Oil for deep-frying

Salt to taste

Place the minced mutton in a bowl, and add the chopped onion, tomato, chopped coriander, green chillies, ginger-garlic paste and salt to taste.

Add the egg, and knead all the ingredients together.

Add the breadcrumbs and divide the mixture into small lime-sized balls.

Heat the oil in a *kadai* and deep-fry 4-5 kebabs at a time, until golden brown. Drain on absorbent paper.

Serve hot with Green Coriander Chutney (page 42), Tomato Chutney (page 22) or *Dhansak* (page 98).

PARSI FIESTA

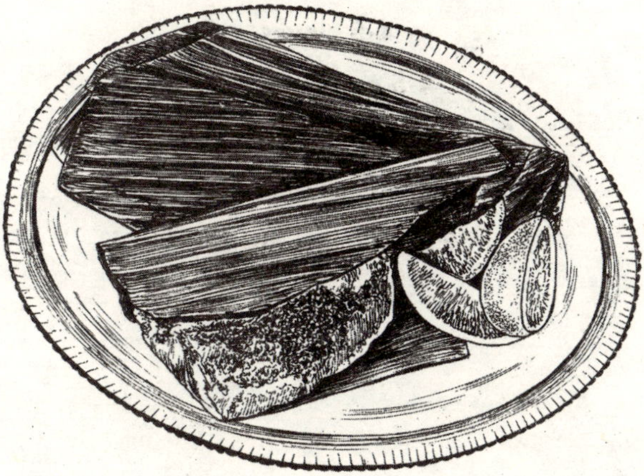

Sample the Parsi penchant for good food with these traditional recipes.

DHANSAK

Brown Rice

1 teaspoon + 2 tablespoons oil
6 teaspoons sugar
2-3 onions, finely chopped
4-5 cloves
4-5 peppercorns
3-4 x 1-inch cinnamon sticks
3-4 cardamoms
2 cups rice, washed
Salt to taste

Heat 1 teaspoon oil in a pan. Add sugar and stir till it caramelises and turns dark brown.

Add 4 cups hot water, stir till the sugar dissolves and set aside.

Heat 2 tablespoons oil in another pan, and fry onions till brown.

Add the cloves, peppercorns, cinnamon, cardamoms, rice and the caramelised sugar water.

Add salt and cook till the rice is done.

Dhansak Dal

1 kg chicken or mutton

1 cup oil-coated split pigeon peas *(toovar dal)*

100 grams split Bengal gram *(chana dal)*

100 grams skinless split green gram *(moong dal)*

100 grams split lentils *(masoor dal)*

2 tablespoons chopped fenugreek leaves *(methi)*

3-4 small brinjals, cut into cubes

50 grams red pumpkin

2-3 tablespoons oil

2-3 large onions, finely chopped

6 teaspoons *dhansak masala* powder

Salt to taste

Cut the chicken or mutton into medium pieces. Cook the chicken with a little water in a pan till half done. For the mutton, add water to cover, and pressure cook till it releases pressure 4 times (4 whistles).

Pressure-cook all the *dal*, fenugreek leaves and vegetables in 3 cups water, till the pressure is released thrice (3 whistles). Remove from heat and cool.

Purée the cooled mixture in a blender to make a thick gravy.

Heat oil in a pan; add onions and *dhansak masala* and fry for 2 minutes. Add the *dal* and partially cooked chicken or mutton with the water in which it was cooked, and cook for another 5 minutes, till the meat is tender.

Serve the *dhansak dal* with Brown Rice (page 98) and Mutton Kebabs (page 96).

SAS-NI-MACHHI

Fish in Spicy White Sauce

2 medium pomfrets (500 grams)

2 tablespoons oil

2-3 medium onions, finely chopped

½ teaspoon cumin seeds

2-3 medium tomatoes, finely chopped

2 tablespoons coriander leaves, finely chopped

1 teaspoon ginger-garlic paste

2-3 green chillies, finely chopped

1 teaspoon refined flour

¼ cup milk

8-10 cherry tomatoes

Salt to taste

For the sauce

2 eggs

¼ cup white vinegar

2 teaspoons sugar

Cut the pomfret into medium slices.

Heat oil in a pan. Add onions, cumin seeds, chopped tomatoes, chopped coriander, ginger-garlic paste and green chillies. Stir for 2-3 minutes.

Sprinkle flour and stir. Add milk and 1 cup hot water and stir to mix well.

Add the fish and salt cook till the fish is done and the *sas* is thick. Add the cherry tomatoes. Remove from the heat and leave to cool.

Beat eggs in a bowl, add vinegar, and sugar, and beat till the sugar dissolves.

Stir gently into the fish and cook on low heat till the gravy thickens further. Do not allow it to boil.

Serve hot with *khichdi*.

CHICKEN COCONUT STEW

2 teaspoons ginger-garlic paste
1 kg chicken, cut into medium pieces
½ coconut, grated
1 cup milk
2 tablespoons oil
2-3 large onions, finely chopped
3 dried Kashmiri chillies, broken into large bits
Salt to taste

Rub the ginger-garlic paste into the chicken and marinate for 1 hour.

Extract coconut milk by blending grated coconut with the milk in a blender. Strain.

Heat oil in a frying pan, and fry the chicken till golden brown. Remove and set aside.

Fry onions and dried chillies in the same oil, till golden brown.

Add the fried chicken and salt. Add coconut milk and cook till tender.

Serve hot, with bread or *chapati.*

Note

You can replace the chicken with ¾ kg mutton.

JARDALOO SALI BOTI

Meat with Dried Apricots and Potato Straws

150 grams dried apricots, stoned
2 tablespoons oil
3 large onions, finely chopped
1 kg boneless mutton, cut into 2-inch pieces
50 grams fried potato straws
Salt to taste

For the masala paste

5-6 dried Kashmiri chillies
3-4 cloves garlic
1 teaspoon cumin seeds
4-5 cardamoms
4-5 x 1-inch cinnamon sticks
4-5 cloves
5-6 black peppercorns
¼ cup brown vinegar

Grind all the ingredients for the *masala* to a smooth paste.

Cook the apricots in water to cover and reserve the water.

Heat oil in a pressure cooker, and fry onions till light brown. Add the *masala* and fry. Add meat and brown on all sides.

Add apricot water and half the apricots and salt and pressure-cook till the pressure is releases 3-4 times (3-4 whistles), and the meat is tender.

Add the remaining apricots and stir.

Garnish with potato straws and serve with *chapati* or bread.

BHARUCHI AKURI

2 tablespoons oil

50 grams raisins

50 grams cashew nuts

2 medium onions, finely chopped

1 large tomato, finely chopped

½ cup coriander leaves, finely chopped

2-3 green chillies, finely chopped

4 eggs

Salt to taste

Heat oil in a *kadai* and lightly fry the raisins and cashew nuts separately. Remove and set aside.

Add onions to the oil and fry till light brown. Add tomato, chopped coriander, green chillies and salt, and stir for 2 minutes.

Break the eggs into this mixture and whisk till the eggs begin to coat the sides of the pan. Add cashew nuts and raisins. Keep stirring till it turns slightly thick.

Serve hot with bread.

FALOODA

5 teaspoons basil seeds *(tukmaria/subja)*

1½ cups milk

1 cup sugar

3 drops pink food colour

3 tablespoons rose syrup

Vanilla ice cream

Soak basil seeds overnight in 1½ cups water.

Bring the milk to a boil and add sugar. Lower heat and simmer, uncovered, for 1 hour. Cool.

Add pink food colour and rose syrup.

Mix the basil seeds into the mixture and chill in the refrigerator for 4 hours.

Serve in chilled glasses with vanilla ice cream.

PARSI RAVA

2 tablespoons semolina

2 tablespoons sugar

1 tablespoon butter

¼ teaspoon vanilla essence

2 cups milk

A few raisins, fried in butter

A few almonds, slivered and fried in butter

Roast semolina on a *tawa*.

Cook semolina, sugar, butter, vanilla essence and milk in a large pan. Stir for a few minutes on low heat till thick.

Pour into glass bowls and sprinkle raisins and almonds.

Chill and serve.

SWEET SENSATIONS

Indulge your sweet tooth or end your meal on a sweet note with these delightful desserts.

CUSTARD SAUCE

2 tablespoons custard powder

½ litre milk

2 tablespoons sugar

Mix together in a small bowl, custard powder with ¼ cup milk till smooth.

Boil the remaining milk in a pan and add the sugar, stirring occasionally, till the sugar is completely dissolved, and remove from heat.

Add the custard mixture to the milk and stir well to prevent lumps from forming.

Cook on low heat, for 2-3 minutes, stirring continuously, until the mixture thickens. Cool.

Makes 2 cups

FRUIT SALAD WITH CUSTARD SAUCE

1 cup CUSTARD SAUCE

Small quantities of a variety of seasonal fruits such as ripe melon, watermelon, papaya, banana, grapes, apple, pear, etc.

Peel, remove the seeds and chop the fruit into medium-sized pieces.

Place the chopped fruit in a bowl, add the custard sauce and mix well.

Refrigerate and serve cold.

Note

You can also serve the chopped fruit with a bowl of custard on the side.

TRIFLE PUDDING

2½ cups CUSTARD SAUCE

250 grams sponge cake, cut into ½-inch thick slices

3 ripe bananas, thinly sliced

150 grams seedless grapes

1 tablespoon pomegranate kernels

Pour enough custard sauce into a deep transparent serving bowl, to cover the bottom.

Place a layer of sponge cake over it.

Add a layer of banana slices and grapes over the cake.

Pour some custard sauce over the fruit.

Place another layer of cake and fruit.

Cover with a layer of custard sauce.

Decorate with pomegranate kernels and refrigerate.

Serve cold.

APPLE CRUMBLE

1 recipe CUSTARD SAUCE

1 kg apples

5-6 tablespoons sugar

50 grams cinnamon

75 grams butter

100 grams refined flour

75 grams cashew nuts or walnuts, crushed

Peel the apples and cut into cubes.

Place in a pan with enough water to cover.

Add sugar and cinnamon, bring to a boil, lower heat and simmer till apples are tender. Cool and remove the cinnamon.

Place apples and syrup in an ovenproof dish.

Preheat the oven to 180°C/350°F/Gas Mark 4.

Make the crumble topping by mixing together lightly the butter, flour and nuts with your fingertips, till the dough resembles coarse sand.

Spoon over the dish of apples till the top is completely covered.

Bake for about half an hour.

Serve hot with custard sauce or chilled with vanilla ice cream.

BAKED CUSTARD

1½ litres milk

4 tablespoons sugar

2-3 eggs

Boil the milk till it thickens and is reduced to half the quantity.

Add sugar. Once the milk is cool, add eggs and stir well.

Preheat the oven to 150°C/300°F/ Gas Mark 2.

Pour into an ovenproof dish and bake for 20 minutes, or till the custard sets.

Cool custard at room temperature and refrigerate.

Serve cold.

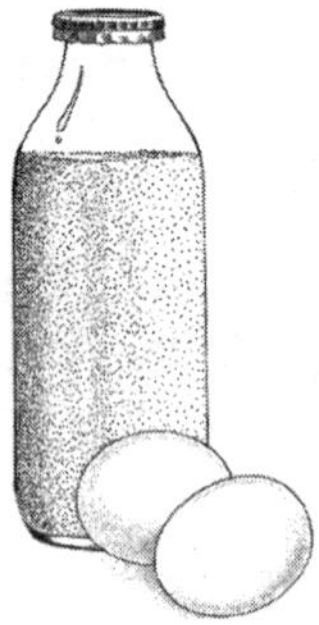

BREAD AND BUTTER PUDDING

1 litre milk

4 tablespoons sugar

3 eggs, beaten

3-4 bread slices

2 tablespoons butter

1 tablespoon raisins

1 tablespoon crushed cashew nuts

Boil the milk in a pan on high heat. Lower the heat and add the sugar, stirring continuously, until the milk reduces to half its original quantity. Cool.

Preheat the oven to 180°C/350°F/Gas Mark 4.

Add beaten eggs to the cooled milk and whisk well.

Cut off the crust of the bread slices and cut each slice into 6 square pieces. Lightly butter the bread pieces.

Arrange the bread slices in an 8-inch square ovenproof dish, and sprinkle the raisins and crushed cashew nuts on top.

Pour the custard mixture over the bread slices.

Bake until the top is golden brown.

Serve hot or cold.

LAGAN-NU-CUSTARD

1½ litres milk

4 tablespoons sugar

2-3 eggs, beaten

1 teaspoon vanilla essence

2 tablespoons rose water

1 tablespoon almonds

1 tablespoon raisins

Boil the milk till it thickens and is reduced to half its original quantity.

Add sugar and stir. Remove from heat and cool slightly. Add eggs and stir well.

Return to heat, add ¼ cup warm water to the mixture, and mix well.

Take the pan off the heat, and add vanilla essence and rose water.

Preheat the oven to 150°C/300°F/Gas Mark 2.

Wash the almonds and place them in hot water for 5 minutes. Cool and remove the skin and cut into slivers.

Add almonds and raisins to the custard mixture and pour into an 8-inch square ovenproof dish.

Bake for 45 minutes, until set and the top is golden brown.

Serve cold.